WHERE TO BEGIN

A SMALL BOOK ABOUT YOUR POWER TO
CREATE BIG CHANGE

WHERE TO BEGIN

CLEO WADE

ATRIA PAPERBACK

New York ♥ London ♥ Toronto ♥ Sydney ♥ New Delhi

ATRIA
PAPERBACK

An Imprint of Simon & Schuster, Inc.
1230 Avenue of the Americas
New York, NY 10020

First Atria Paperback edition April 2020

ATRIA PAPERBACK and colophon are trademarks of Simon & Schuster, Inc.

For information about special discounts for bulk purchases, please contact Simon & Schuster Special Sales at 1-866-506-1949 or business@simonandschuster.com

The Simon & Schuster Speakers Bureau can bring authors to your live event. For more information or to book an event contact the Simon & Schuster Speakers Bureau at 1-866-248-3049 or visit our website at www.simonspeakers.com.

Manufactured in the United States of America

1 3 5 7 9 10 8 6 4 2

Library of Congress Control Number: 2020932163

ISBN 978-1-9821-3879-0
ISBN 978-1-9821-5279-6 (pbk)
ISBN 978-1-9821-3880-6 (ebook)

This is for you.

And me.

And us.

We are the builders who are building a world

that has never been built

before.

Dearest you,

When I started out this year, I had no idea I would write a new book. That was until one day in April I was randomly looking through *Heart Talk* and I opened it up to page 131 where a poem called "Tired" lives. All of a sudden I stopped in my tracks when I saw the line in the poem that read:

I was tired of seeing evil everywhere / so I found the heavenly spots and showed my / neighbors where they were.

When I saw those words, I knew it was time to make a new book. There was a voice within me that said with the utmost urgency that I needed to create a heavenly spot and show my neighbors where it was.

I spent most of last year on the road in community with so many different people, all of whom taught me, inspired me, and made me feel so loved. If you are reading this and were one of the people who came out to any of my tour stops, thank you. You impacted me in ways I can't fully express. As I traveled, there was one question I was asked,

no matter where I went, a big city or a

small town, a room full of fifty people

or a room full of five hundred: it was

"How do you stay sane when it feels like

our world gets crazier and crazier?" Or

if someone asked me for advice on self-

care they would always end the question

with *especially during these times.*

This book is a collection of the ideas,

mantras, and poems I turn to when I

feel like I am losing it. I wrote this so

that I could have them all in one place

when I felt overwhelmed by worry, fear,

anxiety, or helplessness.

The words in this book are what stop me from walking away from the problems of the world during tough times. They also help me stay connected to hope during difficult moments and remind me that even on the days that feel the most daunting, I still have the power to show up and do something, somewhere, in some way.

This book starts with and is named after the poem "Where To Begin," which I originally wrote when I was asked to give a Ted Talk in 2017. I spent a long time thinking about what message was the most important to put into words for the particular moment in history we are living in. I thought about what words carry me through my worst days and what it would look like to put them into a love note for my friends, family, and the next generation (shout-out to Baby Thelonious).

I realized if there was anything that I wanted people to know it was that change-making comes in all sizes. It doesn't always have to be one big gesture or nothing. As my friend Jenna often says, "The big stuff is the small stuff." Your big life is made up of a collection of all your small moments. Our big world is made up of a collection of all our small actions.

Over the past two years since writing that poem, I have found myself returning to it over and over again almost as a meditation when the world around me felt frenzied and I needed to calm my mind and replenish my energy.

The rest of this book is a collection of poems and ideas, some new, some old, as well as some words of advice from friends that I turn to when I need motivation to keep going. This section of the book reminds me that building a beloved community is a lifelong journey, one that requires tools for stamina and self-care.

If there is anything I hope you will walk away with from this book it is that I hope you won't walk away from it at all. I hope you will live with it, write in it, and even color in it. (There are a handful of pages where I outlined the letters so you could fill them in. I personally find coloring to be very relaxing, so I thought I would leave some room in this book for you to share that simple joy with me. I recommend colored pencils or crayons instead of markers.)

I hope that this book can be a heavenly spot for you. I hope this book is one that reminds you that you are powerful and we are going to be okay. And most important, I hope this book makes you feel loved because I love you very much and I am so glad to be in this world with you.

Love,

Cleo

WHERE TO BEGIN

(a poem)*

* this poem takes up the next 91 pages of this book. Reading it out loud
is the most fun (in my opinion), but as always with my work, experi-
ence it however you'd like. Read it front to back, a page a day, pick a
page at random when you feel like it, or color all over it. No rules. This
book isn't mine, it's ours.

THE WORLD WILL SAY

TO YOU:

BE A

BETTER PERSON.

DO NOT

BE AFRAID TO

SAY YES.

cleo wade

START BY

BEING A BETTER LISTENER.

START

BY BEING BETTER

AT WALKING

DOWN THE STREET.

SEE PEOPLE.

SAY HELLO.

ASK HOW THEY ARE DOING

AND

LISTEN TO WHAT THEY SAY

TO YOU.

cleo wade

START BY

BEING

A BETTER FRIEND

A BETTER PARENT

A BETTER CHILD TO YOUR

PARENTS

A BETTER SIBLING

A BETTER LOVER

A BETTER PARTNER.

START BY

BEING

A BETTER NEIGHBOR.

MEET SOMEONE YOU DO

NOT KNOW

AND

GET TO KNOW THEM.

cleo wade

THE WORLD WILL SAY

TO YOU:

WHAT ARE YOU

GOING TO DO?

DO NOT BE AFRAID TO SAY

I KNOW

I CAN'T DO EVERYTHING

BUT

I CAN DO

SOMETHING.

cleo wade

WALK INTO MORE ROOMS, SAYING,

"I'M HERE TO HELP."

BECOME INTIMATE WITH GENEROSITY

GIVE

WHAT YOU CAN GIVE

AND

DO

WHAT YOU CAN DO.

GIVE DOLLARS.

GIVE CENTS.

GIVE YOUR TIME.

GIVE YOUR HEART.

GIVE YOUR SPIRIT.

cleo wade

THE WORLD WILL SAY

TO YOU:

WE NEED PEACE.

FIND YOUR PEACE
WITHIN.

HOLD IT SACRED
BRING IT WITH YOU
EVERYWHERE
YOU GO.

cleo wade

PEACE

CANNOT BE SHARED OR CREATED

WITH OTHERS

IF

YOU CANNOT, FIRST,

GENERATE IT

WITHIN.

THE WORLD WILL SAY

TO YOU:

THEY

ARE THE ENEMY.

cleo wade

LOVE ENOUGH TO KNOW

THAT

JUST BECAUSE SOMEONE

DISAGREES WITH YOU

DOES NOT

MAKE THEM

YOUR ENEMY.

YOU MAY NOT WIN AN

ARGUMENT.

YOU MAY NOT CHANGE

A MIND,

BUT

IF YOU CHOOSE TO . . .

YOU CAN ALWAYS ACHIEVE THE

TRIUMPH OF RADICAL EMPATHY

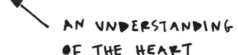

AN UNDERSTANDING
OF THE HEART

THE WORLD WILL SAY

TO YOU:

WE NEED JUSTICE.

INVESTIGATE.

cleo wade

FIND TRUTH

BEYOND

THE STORIES

YOU

ARE TOLD.

FIND TRUTH

BEYOND

THE WAY THINGS SEEM.

cleo wade

ASK:

"WHY?"

ASK:

"IS THIS FAIR?"

ASK:

"HOW DID WE GET HERE?"

DO THIS

WITH

COMPASSION.

DO THIS

WITH

FORGIVENESS.

cleo wade

LEARN TO FORGIVE OTHERS.

START BY

TRULY

LEARNING HOW

TO FORGIVE

YOURSELF.

WE
ARE
ALL MORE
THAN OUR
MISTAKES

WE ARE ALL

MORE

THAN WHO

WE WERE

YESTERDAY.

WE ARE

ALL

DESERVING OF

OUR

DIGNITY.

cleo wade

SEE YOURSELF IN OTHERS

RECOGNIZE

THAT

YOUR JUSTICE

IS

MY JUSTICE

cleo wade

AND MY JUSTICE

IS

YOURS.

THERE CAN BE NO LIBERA-TION FOR

ONE OF US
IF THE
OTHER IS
NOT FREE

THE WORLD WILL SAY
TO YOU:

I AM VIOLENT.

cleo wade

RESPOND

BY SAYING,

I AM NOT.

NOT WITH MY WORDS

AND

NOT WITH MY ACTIONS.

THE WORLD WILL SAY

TO YOU:

WE NEED TO HEAL

THE PLANET.

START BY SAYING,

"NO, THANK YOU, I DON'T NEED A PLASTIC BAG."

RECYCLE.

REUSE.

START BY
PICKING UP
ONE PIECE
OF TRASH
ON YOUR BLOCK.

cleo wade

THE WORLD WILL SAY
TO YOU:

THERE ARE TOO MANY
PROBLEMS.

DO NOT BE AFRAID TO BE A
PART OF THE
SOLUTIONS.

START BY

DISCUSSING THE ISSUES.

cleo wade

WE CANNOT
OVERCOME
WHAT WE
IGNORE

THE MORE WE TALK ABOUT
THINGS,
THE MORE WE SEE
THAT
THE ISSUES
ARE CONNECTED
BECAUSE . . .

cleo wade

WE

ARE

CON-

NECTED▷

THE WORLD WILL SAY

TO YOU:

WE NEED TO END

RACISM.

cleo wade

START BY

HEALING IT

IN YOUR

OWN FAMILY.

THE WORLD WILL SAY
TO YOU:

HOW DO WE SPEAK TO
BIAS AND BIGOTRY?

cleo wade

START BY
HAVING THE FIRST
CONVERSATION
AT YOUR OWN
KITCHEN TABLE.

THE WORLD WILL SAY

TO YOU:

THERE IS TOO MUCH

HATE.

cleo wade

DEVOTE YOURSELF TO LOVE

LOVE YOURSELF

SO MUCH

THAT

YOU CAN LOVE OTHERS

WITHOUT BARRIERS

AND

WITHOUT JUDGMENT.

cleo wade

WHEN THE WORLD ASKS US

BIG QUESTIONS

THAT

REQUIRE BIG ANSWERS,

WE HAVE TWO OPTIONS:

ONE.

TO FEEL SO OVERWHELMED

OR

UNQUALIFIED

WE DO

NOTHING.

cleo wade

TWO.

TO BEGIN.

TO START

WITH ONE SMALL ACT

AND

QUALIFY OURSELVES.

I AM

THE DIRECTOR OF NATIONAL

SECURITY,

AND

SO ARE YOU.

cleo wade

SURE,

NO ONE APPOINTED US AND
THERE WERE NO SENATE
CONFIRMATIONS

BUT

WE CAN

SECURE A NATION.

WHEN WE HELP

JUST ONE PERSON

TO BE MORE SECURE

OUR NATION

IS MORE SECURE.

cleo wade

WITH JUST ONE
OUTSTRETCHED HAND
THAT SAYS,

"ARE YOU OK?
I AM HERE FOR YOU."

WE HAVE

THE POWER

TO TRANSFORM

INSECURITY

INTO

SECURITY.

cleo wade

WE FIND OURSELVES

SAYING TO THE WORLD,

"WHAT DO WE DO?"

"WHAT CAN I DO?"

THE BETTER QUESTION

MIGHT BE,

"HOW AM I SHOWING UP?"

I ASK THE WORLD FOR PEACE

BUT

DO I SHOW UP WITH PEACE

WHEN

I SEE MY FAMILY AND FRIENDS?

I ASK THE WORLD TO PUT A
STOP TO HATRED

BUT

DO I SHOW UP WITH LOVE
FOR NOT ONLY
THOSE I KNOW
BUT
FOR THOSE I DO NOT KNOW?

cleo wade

DO I SHOW UP WITH LOVE

FOR THOSE

WHOSE IDEAS CONFLICT

WITH MY OWN?

I ASK THE WORLD

TO END

SUFFERING,

BUT

DO I SHOW UP

FOR THOSE WHO ARE SUFFERING

ON MY

STREET CORNER?

cleo wade

WE SAY TO THE WORLD:

"PLEASE CHANGE!"

"WE NEED CHANGE!"

BUT HOW DO WE SHOW UP TO

CHANGE OUR OWN LIVES?

HOW DO WE SHOW UP

TO CHANGE

THE LIVES OF THE PEOPLE

IN

OUR COMMUNITIES?

JAMES BALDWIN

SAID,

"EVERYTHING NOW, WE MUST
ASSUME, IS IN OUR HANDS; WE
HAVE NO RIGHT TO ASSUME
OTHERWISE."

AND THIS HAS ALWAYS BEEN
TRUE . . .

NO ONE NOMINATED

HARRIET TUBMAN

TO

HER PURPOSE,

TO

HER COURAGE,

TO

HER MISSION.

cleo wade

SHE DID NOT SAY,

"I AM NOT A CONGRESSPERSON

OR

THE PRESIDENT,

SO HOW COULD I POSSIBLY

PARTICIPATE IN THE FIGHT TO

ABOLISH A SYSTEM

AS BIG AS SLAVERY?"

SHE INSTEAD

SPENT TEN YEARS

MAKING

NINETEEN TRIPS

FREEING

300 PEOPLE,

ONE

PERSON

AT A TIME.

cleo wade

THINK ABOUT THE CHILDREN

OF

THOSE 300 PEOPLE,

THE GRANDCHILDREN,

THE GREAT-GRANDCHILDREN,

AND BEYOND.

OUR RIGH-
TEOUS ACTS
CREATE
IMMEASUR-
ABLE

RIPPLES
IN THE
ENDLESS
RIVER OF
JUSTICE

WHETHER IT WAS

HURRICANE

KATRINA, HARVEY, IRMA,

OR MARIA,

PEOPLE DID NOT SAY,

"THERE'S SO MUCH DAMAGE,

WHAT CAN WE EVEN DO?"

cleo wade

THEY GOT IN THEIR BOATS

AND

STARTED LOADING IN EVERY

WOMAN, MAN,

AND CHILD

THEY CAME ACROSS.

ONE BY ONE

THEY GAVE THEIR DOLLARS,

THEY GAVE THEIR CENTS,

THEY GAVE THEIR TIME,

THEY GAVE THEIR HEART,

AND

THEY GAVE THEIR SPIRIT.

cleo wade

WE SPEND SO MUCH TIME

THINKING

WE DON'T HAVE THE

POWER

TO CHANGE THE WORLD,

WE FORGET THAT THE

POWER

TO CHANGE SOMEONE'S LIFE IS

ALWAYS IN OUR HANDS.

WE ALL HAVE THE

POWER

TO RELIEVE SOMEONE'S PAIN

WITH OUR

EMBRACE.

cleo wade

AND

LESSEN SOMEONE'S SUFFERING

WITH OUR

KINDNESS.

CHANGE-MAKING

DOES NOT BELONG TO ONE GROUP

OF PEOPLE.

cleo wade

CHANGE-MAKING BELONGS TO ALL OF US

YOU DO NOT HAVE TO WAIT FOR

ANYONE

TO TELL YOU

THAT

YOU ARE IN THIS.

cleo wade

YOU DON'T HAVE TO WAIT
AROUND WONDERING WHAT YOU

SHOULD DO

GET TO WORK ON WHAT YOU

CAN DO.

THE TIME HAS ALWAYS BEEN

NOW.

cleo wade

BEGIN.

START BY

DOING WHAT YOU CAN

WITH

WHAT YOU'VE GOT,

WHERE YOU ARE,

AND

IN YOUR OWN WAY.

cleo wade

WE DON'T HAVE TO BE

HEROES,

WEAR A UNIFORM,

CALL OURSELVES ACTIVISTS,

OR

GET ELECTED TO PARTICIPATE.

WE JUST HAVE TO BE

BRAVE

ENOUGH

TO CARE

HOW TO KEEP GOING

(poems and ideas)

how to take the first step on a long journey

first of all
smile
about
what there is
to
smile
about

cleo wade

when moving forward

do not worry
about
feeling lost
there is
a compass
inside of you
if you are listening
it will
tell you
which way to go

BE GOOD TO AS
MANY PEOPLE
AS POSSIBLE.

In January of 2017, my friend Mia
invited me to her grandfather's birthday
in New Jersey. His name is Gene, and it
was his hundredth birthday.

As soon as I walked into the party,
I was overwhelmed by how much joy

cleo wade

and life was in the room. There were grandkids and great-grandkids, pasta and cannoli, laughing and dancing, and even my mother—who is honestly never one to miss a good party—flew in from Louisiana for the celebration.

If you have ever met anyone who has reached a hundred years old, then you know that when you are around them, you can't help but feel like you are in the presence of a miracle. I looked over at Gene toward the end of the night and found myself in awe as I thought about all that he had seen and lived through in his lifetime. As I did the math, I realized that he grew up during the Great Depression, fought in WWII, and had lived through everything from the struggle for worker's rights, to the women's liberation movement, the civil rights movement, a man on the moon, the Vietnam War, and the election of the first black president of the United States, all while sustaining his sixty-six-year marriage to his wife, Maria, who passed in 2014.

Now, right around the time of Gene's birthday, the narrative that America was more divided than ever before was sweeping the nation. It had begun to feel like the only thing any-one could talk about. So, with his life experience in mind, I walked over to Gene, and I asked him if he had any advice during this current time. He looked up for a moment, sat back in his chair, looked back at me, smiled, and said, "Yes. Be good to as many people as possible."

I absorbed those words for a while as I looked around the room at the hun-dreds of people, many of whom had flown thousands of miles to be there, who had gathered from all walks of life to celebrate him. I realized that Gene had not just given me great advice; he had shared with me the first step every single one of us is capable of taking if we want to have a real, wholehearted impact on the world around us:

Be good to as many people as possible. ☉

going somewhere or going nowhere

hate
is a shortcut

love
is the long way

but it is

the only road
that will actually
get you anywhere

go the distance, beloved

something new

your pain made you do that
my pain made me do this
your pain made you hate
my pain made me judge

we get better and better at fighting (each other)
we get better and better at hiding (our feelings)

tell me something

if the old saying is true

and

hurt people hurt people

then

what do

healed people do?

I can't be sure

but
I bet
they heal people

I'm ready
are
you?

cleo wade

We all have pain in our lives and our family lineage. My pain might make me think one way or vote one way on a particular issue; your pain might make you do the opposite. We get so busy doing what my friend Kate calls "shoulding all over each other." (You know what I mean by that—"You should think this" or "You should be doing this" or "You shouldn't be doing that.") We don't take a breath to ask ourselves, what in someone's life experience has influenced their way of moving through the world? What has each of us not healed from yet?

I often hear people say that to resolve our disagreements we need to have "hard conversations." While I don't disagree entirely with that, I do wonder how much more effective our confrontations would be if we focused more on having *healing* conversations.

One day, I was listening to an episode of the podcast *On Being with Krista Tippett*, and her guest was John Lewis, the civil rights leader and congressman, and a personal hero of mine. There was one thing in particular that he said that really moved me. He was discussing the spiritual and psychological exercises that he

cleo wade

and other nonviolent activists would use in the face of the violent racism that they were up against in the 1960s. He said,

> **"We, from time to time, would discuss if you see someone attacking you, beating you, spitting on you, you have to think of that person—years ago, that person was an innocent child, innocent little baby. And so what happened? Something go wrong? Did the environment? Did someone teach that person to hate, to abuse others? So you try to appeal to the goodness of every human being. And you don't give up. You never give up on anyone."**

What does it look like to talk to someone and really see them? Not just the person they are in the current moment, but through all phases of their life. What does it look like to truly believe that we are all born with goodness? What does it look like to never give up on anyone?

When we confront others on our differing views, are we rooting for their healing, or are we focusing on ourselves being right and them being wrong? Are we bringing our most healed self to conflict? The self that is focused on a just *and* peaceful outcome? Are we speaking to people in a way that believes in their ability to change, or in a way that merely shames their position?

Healing conversations are not often easy, but that does not mean they have to be hard conversations. For me, the difference between the two interactions is usually the energy we embody. When our intention is to have a hard conversation, we are generally very harsh and inflexible. But when our intention is to have a healing conversation, our energy is generally a little softer and less judgmental. If we focus on healing, our humanity and hope for the other will always remain intact. Our internal pain often wants to dictate our thoughts, words, and actions, but we always have the power to put the healed spaces within us in charge of our lives, actions, and words instead. ☉

feast on it

your healing
is on its way
to you

have you made
room for
its arrival?

turn on the lights
turn up the music

let it know
that you are home

that you are ready for
your new day

that you believe
your new day belongs
to you

you deserve your healing. feast on it.

SILENCE IS
NOT THE
ANSWER TO YOUR
PAIN.

cleo wade

A few weeks before I finished this book, my friend DeRay walked into my writing room and saw a Post-it note stuck to the bottom of my computer. It read, "Silence is not the answer to your pain." He immediately commented that he felt the note needed to go into this book.

Now, if you have ever been on a tight deadline to finish something, then you know that the last thing you are looking for is someone to tell you to start trying to add more than you planned.

So even though my "suggestion box" wasn't exactly open, I asked him why he felt it was important to include in this text. He said,

> **"I used to think that silence would help the pain go away, that speaking about pain might actually make it worse. But it took me a while to realize that silence doesn't usually help us understand the things that hurt us. Silence, if anything, often makes them hurt more."**

When I was growing up in Louisiana, my brother and I endured so much

cleo wade

racism. We were often the only kids of color in all-white spaces, especially during our high school years. I can't tell you how many times people who were supposed to be our friends made racist comments, cruel jokes, or said the N-word.

I am often asked why I feel that it is important to speak out and use my voice. My answer is always the same: I speak up because I know the pain of being silent.

I remained silent in the face of these hurtful words during my girlhood because I didn't have the language, tools, or courage to speak up. I lived in so much fear that the racist jokes or name-calling would be pointed at me one day, that I spent years hiding in my silence. Too often, as children, teenagers, and even as adults, if we feel outnumbered, or that there is no one to hear us, we feel that speaking up is a privilege that we do not have the ability to access.

As I grew out of my girlhood and into my womanhood, I knew I needed to develop a practice of cultivating the courage to express myself and speak up when I felt like something was wrong.

cleo wade

My first step in doing this was express-
ing myself more in the spaces where I felt
safe. This started with the circle of girl-
friends that I met when I moved to New
York City. As I spoke up more around
my friends, I began to feel less afraid to
express myself in a meeting or in public
spaces.

I realized that the only way that I
could heal the pain of years of being
silent was to be silent no more. I still
get scared and nervous when I speak
out, especially in front of large groups
of people, but whenever I do, I close
my eyes for a moment and repeat this

mantra: "Silence is not the answer to your pain."

I believe that we make the world safer when we speak up. I believe that bravery is contagious and others speak up when we speak up. And perhaps most important, I believe that every time we speak up, we tell the world who we are instead of letting the world tell us who we should be. As I was writing this, I saw a tweet that my friend Katie reposted one day from Melissa McEwan that captured this sentiment perfectly—

"My friend Maud once said, 'There are times when we must speak, not because you are going to change the other person, but because if you don't speak, they have changed you.'"

Silence doesn't change the world. It changes us. It shrinks us. It takes our stories and feelings away from us and buries them alive.

Unearth what is buried within you. Free yourself in this way. ☉

only once

everything is a habit

fear
bravery
loving good
loving badly
speaking up
staying silent
giving
taking
opening up
shutting down
gratitude
ingratitude
building
destroying
doing things kindly
doing things unkindly

which of these habits
are worthy

of this life you will most definitely get to live only
once

how much do you love yours?

I asked her
how she practiced forgiveness?

she looked at me, confused by the question

and said
how much do you love your freedom?

speechless
I stared back at her

she moved in closer to me,
and said,

I love my freedom way too much to live in the
prison of non-forgiveness. How much do you love
yours?

how much do you love your freedom?
how much do you love yours?

THERE IS NOT A SINGLE
CONVERSATION THAT
KINDNESS CANNOT MAKE
INFINITELY BETTER.

cleo wade

Interestingly, the people who often inspire me the most are not those who agree with me, but those who disagree with me with kindness. It is the people who refuse to let me be their enemy just because we have a different perspective or point of view.

Every single one of us has the power to be kind from the beginning of a conversation until the end. Kindness does not mean that we act fake or that we let people walk all over us; it just means that we never allow for any person or situation to turn us into a version of ourselves that we are not proud of.

During the tough moments, when your head is hot, and your patience is almost completely tapped out, try to ask yourself:

> *Can I be kind through this?*
>
> *Can I be kind all the way through this?*
>
> *From beginning to end?*

When we are having trouble showing decency and respect to others it is usually a sign that we need to ask ourselves questions like:

What is actually triggering this un-kindness in me?

Why do I feel like it is not possible for me to express my thoughts or feelings in a way that is kind?

Leading with kindness requires us to work on ourselves and understand that we are responsible for our actions, our reactions, and our inaction. It requires us to spend time getting to know what within us stands in the way of us embodying kindness as we move through the world. It requires us to recognize that no one can force us to act a certain way. How we behave is always on us. Regardless of the other person's behavior, it is still our choice.

Can you remain kind even in the presence of hate? (Especially because it is those who are doing the hating who really need the healing power of kindness in their lives.)

The phrase "Kill them with kindness" seems to continue to be passed to every generation, but it's a phrase, I have to say, I never really liked. Kindness does not kill people; kindness reminds people just how vibrant life can be. Kindness reminds people that a life well lived is

cleo wade

bigger than one particular moment, argument, or disagreement. Kindness reminds people of the best of who we are and who we can be to each other. Give that gift. I promise you, it is a gift that goes a lot further than you could possibly imagine. ☉

inevitabilities

it will get messy (your life)
it will break (your heart)
but
oh, the joy
of all you learn
and the power
you gain
when you figure out
how to clean it up
and make your
heart whole
again
& again
& again & again

cleo wade

know the difference

and if
you have
come
a
long way—

rest

don't stop

AS THE SAYING GOES,
"YOU DIDN'T COME THIS FAR,
JUST TO COME THIS FAR."

we were happy

there is a poem by Hafiz hanging in my house that
reads,

*ever since happiness heard your name, it has been
running through the streets trying to find you.*

it breaks my heart a little every time I look at it.
it makes me think about who we were when we
were young
before things
started getting
explained to us.
things like
gender, race, religion, and sexuality.
things like
fear, rejection, and shame.
before that we were happy
because we hadn't been taught (yet)
not to accept others.
we were happy
because we hadn't been taught (yet)
not to accept ourselves.

every
day
I work to get back to that place

the place where there are no walls between you and me.
the place where
vulnerability is real and beautiful.
the place where
I am happy and you are happy too.

I hear it calling our names.

HOW TO STAY CONNECTED
TO YOUR SOUL:

WHEN SOMETHING HAPPENS IN THE
WORLD THAT IS WRONG, DON'T TRY
TO MOVE ON WITH YOUR LIFE LIKE
IT IS RIGHT. THE VOICE WITHIN YOU
THAT SAYS, "THIS IS NOT OKAY" IS A
DIRECT CALL FROM THE BASIC
GOODNESS OF YOUR SPIRIT. PICK IT
UP. EVERY TIME. PICK IT UP. AND
STAY ON THE LINE UNTIL YOU
FIGURE OUT HOW TO HELP.

cleo wade

Dr. King said,

**"Love is the most durable power
in the world."**

I believe that to be true. And what is
so incredible about this power is that
it is a completely democratized power.
It is available to every single one of us
no matter who we are, where we come
from, or what we have been through.

That's all.

does the sea ever say

does the sea ever say
"I am not the ocean"
and would the river
ever
discriminate
against even
a single
rain drop?
does the pond ever consider the lake
to be anything less
than kin?
and do you think the stream
would ever dream
of feeling inferior to the channel
or the channel ever
regard the stream in any other way
than magnificent in its soothing beauty?

no

it is people who have decided
to categorize themselves
away from each other,
create beliefs to pin themselves
against each other,
and construct hierarchies

in pursuit of
dominance over each other's bodies

all of this
in the name of power

water of course
sighs at these strategies

for
water

knows the true power
of falling
from heaven
and
owning more earth
than
land ever will

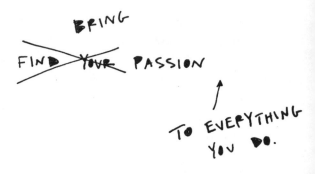

People will tell you to find your purpose.
They will tell you to find your passion.
And I am honestly not sure about that.
We are all such multilayered beings with
an abundance of gifts, talents, inter-
ests, and ideas. Why are we putting the

pressure on ourselves to have one pur-
pose or one passion?

We all grow and shift so much in
our lifetime. Who's to say that your
purpose in your twenties isn't going to
evolve into something else in your thir-
ties, forties, fifties, and beyond?

I have never really felt like I had just
one purpose. And attempting to live life
like I did always felt stressful and inau-
thentic. Instead of concentrating my en-
ergy on one purpose or passion, I try to
focus my energy on what it looks like to
bring passion and purpose to everything
I do.

I do this by asking myself: What type of kindness, care, joy, and patience must I harness in order to bring purpose and passion to my relationship with myself and those around me? What level of openness and curiosity must I own in order to bring meaning to jobs and tasks in my life (even, or especially, the roles that don't spark an immediate sense of excitement within me)?

I don't know anyone who hasn't had jobs that they didn't like on the way to finding the job they do like. I am definitely one of those people. I have babysat, sold t-shirts with photos of crawfish and hot sauce on them to tourists in my hometown, worked in fashion, and as an office manager. None of these jobs were meant for me, but as I went to work answering the phone or pinning a dress, I still tried my hardest to remain curious.

Even on the days where all I wanted to do was pretend to be sick and have a *Gilmore Girls* marathon with my roommate, Molly, I would conjure whatever inner strength I could, show up, and try to continuously look for what that work experience had to teach me.

In fact, I have found that during the moments of doing the things that I liked the least it became the most important to say to myself, "Okay, it's easy to not like this, but what can I learn from it?"

I have also found that our nine-to-five jobs do not have to be how we identify ourselves. They can be, but are not always, the place we feel our greatest sense of purpose or passion. Sometimes a job is just how we pay our bills, which is absolutely fine. And there's nothing wrong with that.

Some of the best advice my friend Grace's dad ever gave us when we were struggling with some of our early jobs was,

"Don't stress about what you have to do during nine to five. Focus on who you are from five to nine."

If you are someone who feels like you know your one true passion or purpose, that is also a wonderful way to go through life, and I am rooting for you every step of your journey. If you are not so sure, I just want you to know that it is okay. Let go of trying to identify yourself by one idea or goal. Instead, commit yourself to bringing purpose and passion into each conversation, workspace, and home space you are a part of. ☺

THIS PAGE

HAS BEEN PLACED IN THIS

BOOK FOR NO OTHER REASON

THAN TO TELL YOU

THAT

YOU ARE DOING JUST FINE.

GIVE YOURSELF A BREAK

AND

START FRESH IF YOU NEED TO

START FRESH.

I LOVE YOU.

　　　　cleo wade

HOW TO CREATE A HEALTHY MEDIA DIET

Food is not the only thing we ingest. We also absorb the energy around us, including what media we allow to be constantly in front of us. One of the best things I ever did for myself was create a media diet that did not trigger my anxiety and insecurities.

This is not to say that I do not keep informed of what is going on in the world or that I hide from the tough stuff in a bubble of privilege; it just means I have boundaries that allow for me to have more of a choice when it comes to how much and what type of content I allow to be a part of my day.

For example, I am very strict about how I get my news. For me, the news has to be about getting information, rather than becoming addicted to different media personalities discussing the information. When I pay too much attention to the commentary that surrounds the news, I often feel like the news is getting worse and worse rather than being able to distinguish that the commentary around it is often just becoming more dramatized.

I find that when I focus on the information and give myself space to reflect on what is happening, I am better able to authentically understand my feelings about the current state of affairs. I am also better able to handle what may emotionally come up based on what I am processing.

My media diet also extends to how I participate in the online world. I find that when I create firm boundaries to only follow social media accounts that share tools, information, and positive imagery, I am less inclined to feel self-conscious, like I'm missing out, or that no matter what I do or have, I will never be enough.

The digital world can be a beautiful

space to build friendships and share ideas, but it can also be pretty toxic depending on how you choose to exist in it.

My boundaries have helped me to see that there is absolutely no person or social media account that is worth making me feel bad about myself. Once I had that realization, it became so easy to unfollow or skip over any content that wasn't right for me.

What are you allowing to be a part of your media diet? Does the way you interact with the media in our world add to or chip away at your emotional stability or sense of self?

Create boundaries that make you feel good and stick to them. Our media surrounds us, whether on a screen in our living room or the palm of our hand, twenty-four hours a day, seven days a week. Learning to manage your relationship with that constant flow of chatter is critical to finding and owning calmness in your life. You are in charge of the amount of commentary and opinions you allow to fill your day and some days you will need to turn it off or log out for a while. It is always okay to disconnect to focus on your mental and emotional health. ☉

MANTRA FOR ANXIETY:
THIS IS NOT YOU. THIS
IS SOMETHING MOVING
THROUGH YOU. IT CAN
LEAVE OUT OF THE
SAME DOOR IT CAME IN.

People often think that because of the
nature of my writing I am always in a
good mood. On the contrary, I have
moved in and out of depressive phases,
have had to lean on friends and family
to help me manage stress more times

than I can count, and struggle to move through feelings of overwhelming anxiety regularly. These life experiences are what inspire most of my writing because it is in those moments that I create words that, similar to a prayer, hold me together when I feel powerless to emotions that are attempting to unravel me. My writing is not about a supernatural ability to avoid hardship, it is about sharing the ideas that keep me together in the midst of it.

I wanted to include my mantra for anxiety in this book because I use it more than anything else I have ever written. It reminds me that my life, my spirit, and my sense of self is bigger than one particular feeling. One rule I have made for myself is to never say that I have anxiety. I always say that I move through anxiety. I do this because I don't want to own an emotional state that blocks me from my personal power. Do I live with waves of anxiety coming in and out of my life? Yes. Do I sometimes need help to cope? Definitely. But am *I* my anxiety? No. I refuse to be. Our identity is rooted in who we are, not how we feel at a given moment. You are more than whatever it is you are going through. ☾

cleo wade

NEVER UNDERESTIMATE
THE POWER OF HOPE—
IT CAN KEEP YOU
WARM ON EVEN THE
COLDEST NIGHT.

In the summer of 2018, my friend Julie invited me to her temple for a conversation between her and psychologist Tal Ben-Shahar. (Fun fact: In the spring of 2006, his course Positive Psychology 1504 became the most popular class in the history of Harvard University.)

The entire talk was amazing, but there was one thing in particular Ben-Shahar said that hit me like a ton of bricks. He said,

> **"The difference between depression and sadness is that depression is sadness without hope."**

For weeks after that talk, his words stayed with me. I thought about hope. I thought about what it looked like to hold on to or have access to hope. His words had suddenly made having a

cleo wade

relationship with hope more important to me than ever before.

A few months later, DeRay Mckesson released his book, *On the Other Side of Freedom,* and in it he created what became my favorite definition of hope. He wrote,

> **"Hope is the belief that our tomorrows can be better than our todays. Hope is not magic; it is work."**

I reflected on this definition for a while. I soon realized that practicing self-care is the first step in our relationship with hope.

When we are not taking care of ourselves, when we are run-down, exhausted, or fed up, we feel defeated. We feel like we are not good enough. We feel like there is something wrong with everything. We feel helpless. We feel cynical, like nothing will ever change. And it is damn near impossible to tap into optimism or hope when we are in this state of mind.

People often look at optimism or hope as character traits that are reserved for people who are either superhuman or completely delusional, but in my experience that is completely untrue.

We earn our optimism.

We earn our hope.

We do this by caring for ourselves mentally, emotionally, spiritually, and physically so that when we show up in the world, we are able to show up with the best of what is within us.

When we show up as a person who is cared for and loved, we have the energy and ability to approach the world's problems with optimism and hope. When we are cared for, we are in the best possible headspace and heart space to find solutions for our communities that are kind, humane, just, moral, and ethical.

No matter what your day looks like, I encourage you to find a moment to give yourself care. Self-care is more than a trend or a set of products someone is trying to sell us. Self-care is how we claim peace of mind. When we know how to gift peace to our inner world, the pathway to creating peace in the world around us is so much clearer. When we approach our community as our most cared for and loved self, we are able to offer divine healing, joy, and solutions to those around us. I can't think of anything better to share with our community.

holding on to it

hope
got a little harder
today

still

I cannot let
these types of days
rob me
of my faith in

humanity

for it
is
these types of days

I need it the most

how to breathe when you want to give up

today I am breathing through fatigue, fear, and feeling overwhelmed.

I breathe because when I breathe, I am reminded that I am alive.

I am reminded that to be able to fill my body with air means that I have the ability to keep going.

I am reminded that my time on earth may be short but it can be powerful if I dedicate it to love and fairness.

when I breathe
I am reminded of Mary Oliver when she wrote,

"tell me, what is it you plan to do with your one wild and precious life?"

so I breathe
and let my breath
turn into a smile that says back to her,

"as much as I can."

one more thing

if all of your
dreams
came true
would they just change you?
or
would they change the world?

*dream bigger, loved ones. bigger, and wider, and
deeper, and further.*

NOTES FOR YOUR BEGINNING

(a space for you to finish this book)

WHOEVER YOU ARE
WAITING ON . . .

STOP WAITING
ON THEM.

CHANGE STARTS
WITH YOU.

---

your name here

notes for your beginning

your name here

notes for your beginning

your name here

notes for your beginning

your name here

notes for your beginning

your name here

notes for your beginning

your name here

_____

_____

_____

_____

_____

_____

_____

_____

_____

_____

_____

_____

_____

_____

_____

_____

_____

_____

_____

_____

_____

notes for your beginning

your name here

notes for your beginning

your name here

notes for your beginning

your name here

Freedom is never really won.
You earn it and win it in
every generation.

Coretta Scott King

Acknowledgments

To everyone who allows my work to be a part of their life, thank you. I treasure it. I treasure you and I am so grateful for your support over the years.

There is not a single person who spent more time working on this book with me than Eleanor Vernon. E, you made this book happen. Thank you.

Thank you also to Dana Sloan for the endless hours of work and care you put into this book.

To Cait Hoyt, thank you for being the most incredible co-dreamer on this journey.

Simon, thank you for pushing me, supporting me, and loving me so well. I am eternally grateful that I get to share my life with you.

To all of the Ancestors: the artists, makers, writers, thinkers, and activists that fought for my existence to be possible, thank you. I promise to get up every day and try to use my one life to make you proud.